Saskatchewan

T 111114

Saskatchewan

Gillian Richardson

Lerner Publications Company

LIBRARY OF CONGRESS
CATALOGING-IN-PUBLICATION DATA

Richardson, Gillian.
    Saskatchewan/by Gillian Richardson
        p. cm. —(Hello Canada)
    Includes index.
    ISBN 0–8225–2760–X (lib. bdg.)
    1. Saskatchewan—Juvenile literature. 2. Saskatchewan.
I. Title. II. Series.
F1071.4.R53 1995
971.24—dc20   94-44842
                                               CIP
                                                AC

Cover photograph by Karpan Photo. Background photo by R. Chen/SuperStock.

The glossary on page 68 gives definitions of words shown in **bold type** in the text.

Senior Editor
Gretchen Bratvold
Editor
Elizabeth Weiss
Photo Researcher
Cindy Hartmon
Series Designer
Steve Foley
Designer
Michael Tacheny

Our thanks to Bernice Barbara Pasmeny, Extension Director at the Saskatchewan History and Folklore Society, for her help in preparing this book.

Manufactured in the United States of America
1 2 3 4 5 6 – JR – 00 99 98 97 96 95

 This book is printed on acid-free, recyclable paper.

Contents

Fun Facts

🍁 Nicknamed Canada's Breadbasket, Saskatchewan is the nation's leading producer of wheat.

🍁 Regina, Saskatchewan's capital city, used to be called Pile of Bones because a huge mound of buffalo skeletons once littered the area.

🍁 Sunshine lovers soak up lots of rays in Estevan, Saskatchewan—Canada's sunniest city. Here the sun shines an average of 2,540 hours annually. That means clear skies for more than half the year!

Hi! My name is Barkley. As you read *Saskatchewan*, I will be helping you make sense of some of the maps and charts that appear in the book.

🍁 Swimmers don't have to worry about sinking in Saskatchewan's Little Manitou Lake. The water is so salty—three times saltier than any ocean—that people easily stay afloat without using inner tubes.

🍁 Fossil remains of a mighty *Tyrannosaurus rex* were discovered in the badlands of southwestern Saskatchewan in 1991. Workers at the site hope to eventually unearth the entire skeleton of the dinosaur.

🍁 Saskatchewan is home to North America's oldest bird **sanctuary.** Here many kinds of birds such as pelicans, ducks, and Canada geese are safe from hunters. The sanctuary was established in 1887.

Two boys wade through a bright yellow field of canola plants, whose seeds are used to make cooking oil. Tall grain elevators (inset) *rise above Saskatchewan's grasslands.*

8

Wide Open Spaces

Grain elevators—tall structures for storing wheat—are visible for miles on the wide open prairies of Saskatchewan, one of Canada's three Prairie Provinces. The **prairies,** or grasslands, that spread across southern Saskatchewan contain rich soil used for growing wheat crops. As the supplier of more than half of Canada's wheat, Saskatchewan is often called the Wheat Province.

Saskatchewan sits between the two other Prairie Provinces, with Alberta to the west and Manitoba to the east. The Northwest Territories borders Saskatchewan to the north. The U.S. states of Montana and North Dakota lie to the south.

On a map of Canada, Saskatchewan is shaped like a tall rectangle, with all its boundaries drawn as straight lines. In fact, Saskatchewan is the only Canadian province that doesn't have any borders formed by natural features such as rivers or a coastline. As for size, the European countries of France and Greece together could almost fit inside the province.

Thousands of years ago, massive sheets of thick ice called **glaciers** inched across what is now Saskatchewan, exposing bare rock in the northern areas. Like gigantic bulldozers, the ice sheets gouged the earth, pushing the best soil southward.

In the Canadian Shield, one of Saskatchewan's three natural land regions, the glaciers uncovered some of the oldest rock in the world. They also

Spruce trees grow in the Canadian Shield region.

carved many hollows that eventually filled with rainwater and melting ice to form lakes and bogs. Nowadays spruce and birch trees take root in this rugged region, which spreads across the northern third of the province. The thick forests are home to black bears, wolves, moose, elk, caribou, and beavers.

Northern residents hunt and trap some of these animals as a source of food and income. In the small communities that dot the region, many people make a living from mining or logging. Indians in the area harvest and sell wild rice and wild blueberries.

Another region, the Plains, stretches across central and southern Saskatchewan. Most of the province's cities and towns—including the capital—are scattered throughout the Plains. Low, rolling hills and deep river valleys extend across the central part of the Plains. To the south, the region is mainly flat prairie.

Farmers grow high-quality grain crops in the rich prairie soil. Some of the soil is a heavy clay mixture, known as gumbo, that holds moisture and minerals well. Beneath the prairie soil lie other important resources, such as oil, natural gas, and potash (a mineral used to make fertilizer).

A prairie dog stands as a lookout, ready to jump back into its hole at the first sign of danger.

11

SASKATCHEWAN
Political Map

| 0 | 75 | 150 | 225 km |
| 0 | 50 | 100 | 150 mi |

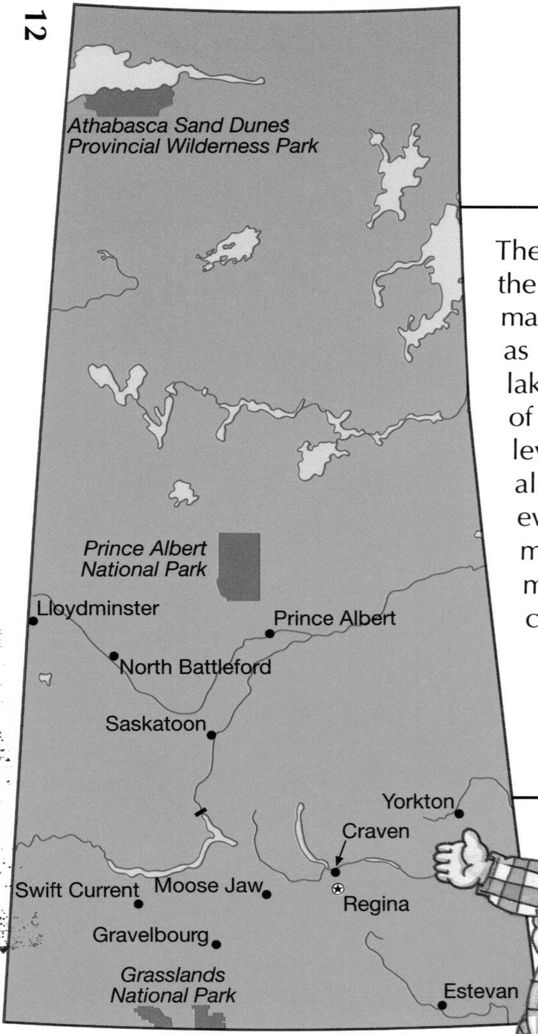

The drawing of Saskatchewan on the facing page is called a physical map. It shows physical features such as highlands, flatlands, rivers, and lakes. The colors represent a range of elevations, or heights above sea level (see legend box). This map also outlines each of Saskatchewan's geographic regions. The map to the left, called a political map, mainly locates features created by people, which may include cities, railways, and parks.

Athabasca Sand Dunes
Provincial Wilderness Park

Prince Albert
National Park

Lloydminster

North Battleford

Saskatoon

Prince Albert

Yorkton

Craven

Regina

Estevan

Swift Current   Moose Jaw

Gravelbourg

Grasslands
National Park

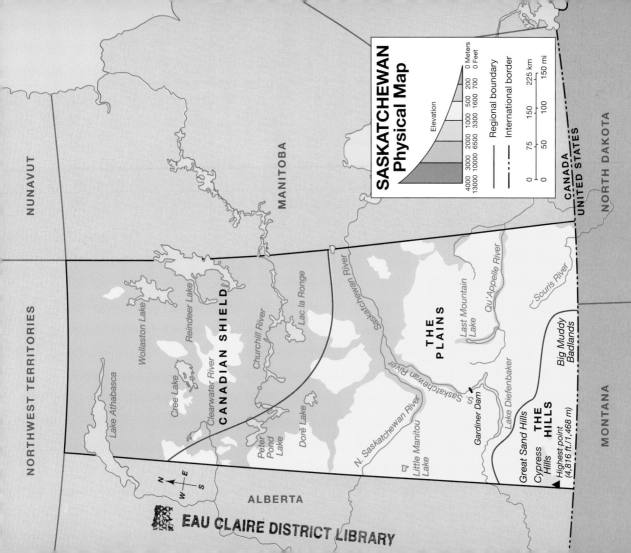

SASKATCHEWAN Physical Map

Elevation

Meters	Feet
0	0
200	700
500	1600
1000	3300
2000	6500
3000	10000
4000	13000

—— Regional boundary

–··– International border

| km | 0 | 75 | 150 | 225 |
| mi | 0 | 50 | 100 | 150 |

NUNAVUT

NORTHWEST TERRITORIES

MANITOBA

CANADA
UNITED STATES

NORTH DAKOTA

MONTANA

ALBERTA

Lake Athabasca

Wollaston Lake

Reindeer Lake

Cree Lake

Clearwater River

Churchill River

Lac la Ronge

CANADIAN SHIELD

Saskatchewan River

Peter Pond Lake

Doré Lake

N. Saskatchewan River

Little Manitou Lake

S. Saskatchewan River

Gardiner Dam

Lake Diefenbaker

THE PLAINS

Last Mountain Lake

Qu'Appelle River

Souris River

Great Sand Hills

Cypress Hills

THE HILLS

Big Muddy Badlands

▲ Highest point (4,816 ft./1,468 m)

N E S W

The province's third region, the Hills, is in the southwestern corner of Saskatchewan. Here the forested Cypress Hills reach to 4,816 feet (1,468 meters)—marking the highest point between Labrador, in eastern Canada, and the Rocky Mountains to the west. North of the Cypress Hills are the Great Sand Hills, where visitors can climb sand dunes, or ridges of sand piled high by the wind. To the east lie the Big Muddy Badlands, which feature scenic

In southern Saskatchewan, rolling prairie grasses give way to the lush Cypress Hills (left). *To the east, bandits used to hide among the rough hills of the Big Muddy Badlands* (opposite page). *Nowadays this wild landscape is a popular spot for tourists and nature lovers.*

hills sculpted by wind and rain. This dry, dusty landscape has few plants.

Although parts of southern Saskatchewan are very dry, some large rivers flow across the region. The Saskatchewan River enters the province from the west in two branches—the North Saskatchewan and the South Saskatchewan. They join just east of the city of Prince Albert. Along the South branch, the Gardiner Dam forms Lake Diefenbaker. Water from this artificial lake is used to produce **hydropower,** which brings electricity to homes and businesses in the province. The lake also provides water for farmers on the southern prairies to use to irrigate their fields.

The Qu'Appelle and the Souris Rivers run through southeastern Saskatchewan. In the Canadian Shield, the Churchill River flows eastward through a chain of glacial lakes. The river's swift rapids and falls challenge daring canoeists.

Reindeer and Wollaston Lakes, Lac la Ronge, and Lake Athabasca are major bodies of water in the north. On the southern shore of Athabasca—the province's largest lake—sits a desertlike area of huge, ancient sand dunes.

Fewer lakes are found in the Plains region. Last Mountain Lake, north of Regina, is one of the region's biggest. Many little lakes called **potholes** were carved out by the glaciers and later filled with rain and melting snow.

Along Lake Athabasca lie some of North America's largest sand dunes.

Sandpipers and pintail ducks nest in these potholes, which also serve as rest stops for endangered birds such as whooping cranes. Hawks and eagles prey on the province's red foxes, jackrabbits, and prairie dogs.

16

Pronghorn antelope and mule deer nibble on the province's prairie grasses. Huge herds of bison, or buffalo, once thundered across Saskatchewan's prairies. Nowadays small herds are protected in sanctuaries.

A colorful mallard duck (above) *basks in the sunshine. In some parts of the province, bird-watchers have counted more than 100 bird species in just one outing. Nature lovers exploring the northern forests might catch a glimpse of a shy white-tailed deer* (right).

The flaming petals of the western red lily, the provincial flower, stand out against a green background.

Prairie summers are short but hot. Sometimes severe hailstorms hit fast, damaging crops and property. In the north, residents enjoy warm days and cool nights during summer. Saskatchewan's average temperature during the season is 64° F (18° C).

Winter in Saskatchewan is long and cold, with an average temperature of 0° F (–18° C). Bitterly cold winds blow across the open prairie, and blizzards sometimes close the highways. During the season, northern residents often travel on roads that cross the region's frozen lakes. Even big trucks hauling supplies use these temporary paths, which vanish during spring thaw.

Saskatchewan gets about 16 inches (41 centimeters) of **precipitation** (rain and melted snow) each year. Less than 12 inches (30 cm) of rain and snow fall in the far north and the southwest annually, so these areas are very dry.

Many people like Saskatchewan's dry, sunny climate. But because the weather can change in a hurry, they keep a close eye on the sky!

Sled dogs race across Saskatchewan's winter landscape.

Tracking Buffalo and Beavers

Around 12,000 years ago, hunters in what is now Saskatchewan used stone weapons to kill game animals, such as giant sloths and mammoths. Thousands of years later, other Aboriginals, or Indians, in the area stalked buffalo for meat and hides. These hunters hurled spears at their prey. Over time, their descendants continued to track buffalo.

By A.D. 800, Aboriginals in what is now Saskatchewan were using bows and arrows to hunt. The Indians also made pottery and tools. Some of the Indian groups in the area included the Chipewyan, Blackfoot, Assiniboine, and Cree nations.

Looking into the Past

Many Aboriginal groups tell stories of how they came to be. In Cree myths, for example, the Creator made people but grew angry when they fought among themselves. The Creator then flooded the earth, sweeping away everything but a few animals. They dove deep beneath the water looking for a kernel of leftover soil. On this piece of dirt, the land returned and became home to new people and animals. By handing down legends from generation to generation, Indians keep their history alive.

Indians on the prairie hunted herds of buffalo (above) *for food. The people recorded scenes from their lives in rock paintings called pictographs* (inset).

Early Chipewyan lived in the far northeastern forests. These Indians fished and hunted moose and caribou. Using well-crafted snowshoes and sleds, the Chipewyan traveled across the snowy wilderness to find game. They made animal hides into tents, clothing, and bags for carrying snowshoes.

Farther south, Blackfoot, Cree, and Assiniboine peoples trekked across the open prairie in search of food. Known as Plains Indians, these groups mainly depended on buffalo but also gathered roots, berries, and wild plants to eat. Hunters drove buffalo herds over cliffs, then speared the injured animals below.

The Indians used every part of the buffalo. They ate the meat fresh or dried and pounded it to make pemmican, a food that also included berries and animal fat. The Plains Indians sewed the buffalo hides to make clothing and cone-shaped dwellings called tepees. Bones were crafted into needles, knives, and spears.

Indian groups had the vast plains and forests to themselves until the late 1600s. At that time, the British Hudson's Bay Company sent Henry Kelsey, a fur trader, to explore the region.

The company had claimed the right to trade on all the land whose rivers drained into a large inland sea in northeastern Canada called Hudson Bay. This huge trading area, named Rupert's Land, included territory in what is now Saskatchewan.

Tepees (below) **were easy to take apart and carry, so Plains Indians could easily move their homes when following herds of buffalo.** *Chipewyan Indians relied on meat and skins from caribou* (left). **The antlers were carved to make spears and fish hooks.**

Henry Kelsey was the first European to see the prairies of what is now Saskatchewan.

The British mainly wanted beaver furs, which were made into hats in Europe. British traders relied on Indians to trap the animals and to bring the furs to British posts. In exchange, the Indians received scissors, hatchets, cloth, guns, and other manufactured goods.

After reaching what is now Saskatchewan in 1691, Kelsey encouraged the Plains Indians to bring beaver pelts to Hudson Bay. But the long inland distances were hard to travel. The Indians didn't agree to Kelsey's plan.

French fur traders also wanted to bargain with Indians in what is now Saskatchewan. In the 1730s, a Frenchman named Louis-Joseph Gaultier de La Vérendrye explored stretches of the Saskatchewan River. Soon French traders had set up trading posts along the waterway, in the Indians' homelands.

Angered by the competition, Britain sent explorer Anthony Henday to what is now Saskatchewan in 1754. Plains Indians guided him along the Saskatchewan River into their territory. Henday couldn't convince them to travel far from home to bring furs to the British. The Indians already had all they needed for survival.

Soon independent fur traders began to bargain with the Indians on the plains. To try to gain a stronger foothold in the region, the Hudson's Bay Company sent Samuel Hearne to start a trading post near the Saskatchewan River. Built in 1774, Cumberland House became Saskatchewan's first permanent European settlement.

Many of the European traders married Aboriginal women. Their children, known as Métis, shared the languages and traditions of both parents. The Métis played a big role in the fur trade, supplying white traders with pelts or pemmican.

Samuel Hearne

Hudson's Bay Company posts were set up like stores. After Indian trappers dropped off furs, they could choose from a variety of European goods such as blankets, rifles, and metal cooking pots.

Aboriginals involved in the fur trade supplied traders with pelts and buffalo meat. Among the items the Indians bargained for was alcohol, a drink they were not used to. Under the influence of rum and wine, many Indians were easily cheated by traders.

Contact with the Europeans also brought new diseases, such as smallpox and measles, to the Indians. Aboriginals had never before been exposed to these illnesses. By the late 1700s, thousands of Indians had died.

By this time, the independent fur traders had formed the North West Company. This trading firm competed with the Hudson's Bay Company until 1821, when the two groups joined. This new and bigger firm, which kept the name Hudson's Bay Company, controlled the fur trade for many years.

Settling the West

John Palliser

In the mid-1800s, big changes took place farther east. Political leaders in what are now Ontario, Québec, New Brunswick, and Nova Scotia came together to form a new country. They signed the British North America Act of 1867, creating the Dominion of Canada.

In 1857 British leaders wanted to find out if it would be a good idea to encourage settlers to build farms on the western prairies. So Britain sent an explorer named Captain John Palliser to examine the prairie soil. Was it good enough for farming?

The Palliser expedition lasted almost three years. Although he was impressed by the lush Cypress Hills in what is now Saskatchewan, Palliser reported that most of the surrounding areas were too dry for farming. As it turns out, he was right and wrong. The soil that he inspected was dry and acidic—not the best type to nourish plants. But much of the land that Palliser explored more than 100 years ago was eventually irrigated by Canadian farmers and became good ground for cattle ranches and wheat fields.

Wanting more territory, the Canadian government bought Rupert's Land from the Hudson's Bay Company. Parts of Rupert's Land, along with lands farther west, were renamed the North-West Territories. This vast area included what is now Saskatchewan.

Soon newcomers from the eastern Canadian provinces headed to the territory to start new lives. At the same time, many **immigrants** arrived from the United States and Europe. To attract more settlers, Canadian officials offered free land to people who promised to farm, build homes, and establish towns.

Immigrants plowed the grasslands to plant crops.

Some of the people who crossed the U.S. border headed north to the plains. They were searching for a good source of buffalo hides. The U.S. traders bargained with Blackfoot and Cree Indians. Soon the two Indian groups were fighting over hunting territory. With so much demand for buffalo hides, the herds shrank quickly.

U.S. and Canadian hunters clashed with a group of Assiniboine during the spring of 1873. Searching for their stolen horses in the Cypress Hills, the hunters got into a disagreement with some Assiniboine camped nearby. Shots were fired, and 30 Indians and one Canadian lost their lives in what is known as the Cypress Hills Massacre.

Hoping to halt the spread of violence in the west, the Canadian government founded the North-West Mounted Police (Mounties) that same year. These lawmen were sent to the prairies on horseback. Their job was to keep the peace as new settlers arrived.

Newcomers to the prairies described the Cypress Hills as an island of forest in a sea of grass.

29

LAW AND ORDER

In 1874 the North-West Mounted Police headed out across the prairie in their bright red coats, determined to make the west a safe and orderly place. Known as Mounties, the strong, disciplined soldiers probably had no idea what the journey really held in store.

Crossing the lonely, unfamiliar prairie was dangerous. Along the way, the soldiers suffered from hunger and from the summer heat. Swarms of mosquitoes hovered over the trail. Horses grew weak from lack of water. Some men deserted the force, but those who stayed learned to survive in rough conditions. After the miserable month-long journey, the Mounties reached their destination.

The North-West Mounted Police set up posts in the Cypress Hills and in surrounding areas. With help from Indian and Métis scouts and interpreters, the Mounties brought law and order to the west. Earning respect and a reputation for fairness, the North-West Mounted Police became legendary figures in Canadian history.

To open more land for settlers, the Canadian government promised the Indians money, education, and medical help if they would sign **treaties** (agreements) giving up claim to the land. The Aboriginals would have to settle on **reserves,** or territories set aside specifically for Indians. These treaties seemed strange to the Indians, who believed that the land was sacred and that no one had the right to own it.

But many Indians, sick or dying from European diseases, needed medical attention. Many others were starving because their main food source, the buffalo, had been wiped out by this time. The Indians saw no choice but to agree to the government's plans, if they were to survive.

Meanwhile, settlers continued to arrive. They came to farm the land or to lay railroad tracks across western Canada. Many of the railroad workers were immigrants from China. Soon the Canadian Pacific Railway chugged across the prairie, bringing even more settlers.

These newcomers put down roots in the growing prairie towns that lay along the railway. Moose Jaw, Saskatoon, and Yorkton quickly became important cities. Regina, just a small town before the coming of the railroad, was named the territorial capital in 1883.

People who made their homes on the prairie didn't have an easy life. The climate was harsh, and the days were lonely since few settlers had close neighbors. Long stretches of land lay between the settlers and the nearest town.

The Soddie

Settlers faced a hard problem when they arrived on the treeless prairie—how to build a house with no logs. The answer was sod, the thick mat of tough prairie grass and tangled roots that held the soil together.

Houses made of sod were called soddies (*above*). For walls, builders piled up slabs of sod, leaving space for a door and some windows. By covering these openings with animal hides or empty flour sacks, the settlers kept out the fierce wind. The floors were nothing but packed dirt.

On rainy days, some sod roofs leaked, turning the floor to mud. Sometimes bugs and other creatures wriggled in through the walls. But the soddies stayed snug in winter and cool in summer and gave the settlers a place to call home.

The Métis feared these new settlers. Many Métis had farms along the Saskatchewan River and were worried that white settlers would take over their land. After asking for help from the Canadian government, the Métis were told they had no official claim to their land.

The government also ignored requests from Indians for help. Hunger and disease were spreading quickly through the Indian reserves.

Many Métis hunted, farmed, and traded for a living. The traders often hauled furs and other goods in Red River carts. These wooden vehicles, pulled by work animals, had large wheels that squeaked loudly while rolling across the prairie.

The Métis and the Indians tried to work peacefully with the government. But when their efforts failed, they turned to force. In 1885 Métis leader Louis Riel set up a Métis government in the settlement of Batoche. He then led a successful fight against the Mounties. Meanwhile, to get food, Indians left the reserves and raided stores owned by white settlers.

In response to the conflict, the Canadian government sent more troops. Some of the Mounties headed to Batoche, where they battled the Métis. Other troops, sent to stop the Indians, clashed with Cree fighters led by Chiefs Poundmaker and Big Bear.

The Mounties won what became known as the North-West Rebellion. The defeated Indians returned to the reserves, and Poundmaker and Big Bear went to jail. Louis Riel was put on trial in Regina, found guilty of treason (betraying the government), and hanged.

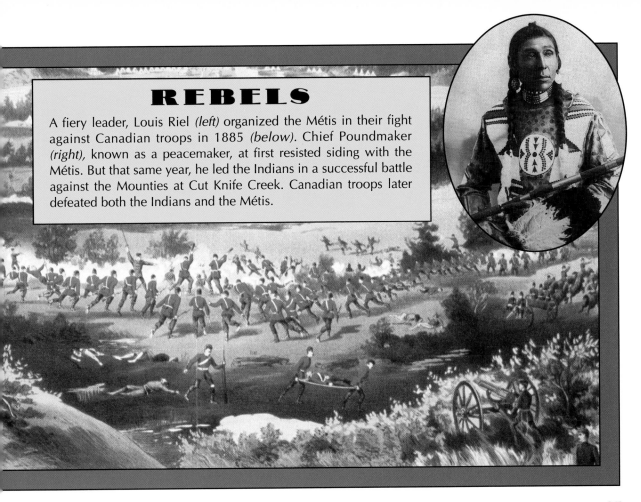

REBELS

A fiery leader, Louis Riel *(left)* organized the Métis in their fight against Canadian troops in 1885 *(below)*. Chief Poundmaker *(right)*, known as a peacemaker, at first resisted siding with the Métis. But that same year, he led the Indians in a successful battle against the Mounties at Cut Knife Creek. Canadian troops later defeated both the Indians and the Métis.

After the rebellion, the Canadian government promoted settlement of the west. Welcoming the chance to own land, Hungarian, German, Swedish, Ukrainian, and Icelandic immigrants traveled by ship to eastern Canada, then completed the long journey westward by train. The newcomers plowed the prairies to grow wheat crops. By the early 1900s, the population of what is now Saskatchewan was booming.

The growing territory soon needed schools and hospitals. But to obtain enough money from the government to help pay for teachers and doctors, the territory had to join Canada as a province. In 1905 the government carved two new provinces—Saskatchewan and Alberta—from the North-West Territories. Saskatchewan took its name

In the summer of 1912, disaster hit Regina. A cyclone (wind storm) swept across the city, killing 28 people and crumpling buildings. Thousands of residents lost their homes.

from the Cree word *Kis-is-ska-tche-wan,* meaning "swift-flowing river."

By this time, farmers in Saskatchewan were growing huge amounts of high-quality wheat. They used machines instead of animals to help harvest the grain. But in the early 1920s, wheat prices fell. By 1924 farmers had formed the Saskatchewan Wheat Pool, an organization that sold wheat directly to other countries and split the profits among members. The Wheat Pool helped farmers throughout the province earn a better living.

Hard times hit Saskatchewan during the Great Depression of the 1930s. During this worldwide economic slump, grain prices fell, factories and businesses closed, and workers were laid off. The bad times got worse when a **drought,** or period with no rain, hit soon after.

Wind whipped up the dry soil, creating huge dust storms during the drought. Crops could barely survive under these conditions, and big swarms of grasshoppers ate the few plants that did grow. These terrible years on the prairies are remembered as the Dirty Thirties.

In 1935 a group of about 1,000 men boarded a train in western Canada and headed east to Ottawa, the nation's capital. They planned to voice their anger about Canada's economic troubles to government leaders. Along the way, many other people joined the men. When the train stopped in Regina, Mounties and city police officers tried to arrest the leaders of the angry group. A huge fight quickly broke out. One policeman died, and many people were injured in what is known as the Regina Riot.

During World War II, men and women in Saskatchewan made weapons in the province's factories.

World War II (1939–1945) helped the province recover. The demand for wheat rose, so Saskatchewan's farmers earned more money. These growers supplied grains and meat to soldiers who were fighting overseas. After the war, immigrants from war-torn countries flooded into Saskatchewan.

In 1944 a political party known as the Co-operative Commonwealth Federation (CCF) came to power in Saskatchewan. Led by Tommy Douglas *(above)*, the CCF party supported socialism—a system where the government, rather than private citizens, manages the economy, health care, and other services. Douglas stayed in office for 17 years. His was the first socialist government in North America.

At about the same time, people in Saskatchewan began improving their government programs. Workers in the provincial government started many services for residents. For example, a province-wide health insurance plan was set up in 1947 to pay the costs of people's hospital care. By the 1960s, this program had expanded and was called Medicare. Medicare allowed all residents of Saskatchewan to get free medical help. The other Canadian provinces eventually adopted this plan, too.

Indians and Métis in the province also have worked to make their voices heard in the government. They have formed organizations to help improve their lives and to preserve their languages and heritage. In 1992 Indian groups in Saskatchewan gained more reserve land by proving that old land treaties hadn't been honored.

Saskatchewanians from all backgrounds are hopeful about the future. The early settlers learned that it took hard work to make a living from the land. Nowadays their descendants, when facing harsh weather or low earnings, still say, "Wait until next year." They know bad spells don't last forever.

Officials pass laws in the Legislative Building in Regina.

Saskatchewan's farmers raise beef and dairy cattle on ranches in the Plains region.

The Wheat Province

Saskatchewan's natural resources are the basis for many jobs. For example, miners in the province unearth precious metals and drill for oil. Loggers harvest trees in Saskatchewan's forests. At manufacturing plants around the province, workers turn these natural resources into products. Other people transport or sell the goods.

But the most important natural resource in Saskatchewan is soil. Saskatchewan has more farmland than any other province. Farmers sell their agricultural products to places all over the world, including the United States, Europe, and Japan.

Seeds from sunflowers are used to make snack foods and vegetable oil.

Wheat is the province's major crop, but canola, flaxseed, and barley are important, too. The province counts on earnings from sunflowers, canary seed, and mustard seed during years when wheat prices are low. Some farmers in Saskatchewan plant potatoes and other vegetables or raise beef and dairy cattle, hogs, and chickens. Altogether, farmers make up about 19 percent of Saskatchewan's workforce.

Saskatchewan's farmers spend a lot of money on machinery, on fertilizers, and on **insecticides** that kill unwanted insects. Insecticides have an added cost—their chemicals can seep into the earth, harming the soil and the water that lies underground. Many of the chemicals are poisonous to animals and people. So researchers are working to help farmers grow high-quality crops using fewer chemicals.

Farming in Saskatchewan is strongly affected by the weather. Grain farmers need about 100 frost-free growing days to produce healthy crops. And farmers constantly check the amount of rainfall—not wanting too much or too little. Sometimes hail or severe winds sweep across fields, damaging plants. Droughts, grasshoppers, or plant diseases also can wipe out a crop.

Whether farmers in Saskatchewan have a good or bad year, other workers in the province feel the effects. For example, service employees, who help people and businesses, may have jobs that relate to agriculture. They might sell and repair farm equipment or operate grain elevators. When farm earnings are down, fewer of these services are needed. And when earnings are up, business improves for the service companies.

Many farmers in the province use large machinery for planting seeds and spreading fertilizer.

HARVESTTIME

During fall, farmers in southern Saskatchewan anxiously wait for weather reports. Will the frost hold off? The farmers watch as the wheat fields turn yellow and the tops of the plants become firm—it's harvesttime!

Harvesting is hard labor. Farm families often work long days and well into the night to get the job done. First they must swath, or cut, the wheat and let it lie in the fields to dry for about a week. Snow or hard rain during this week can ruin the crop. Families hope for dry, windy weather.

Next the farmers drive a large machine called a combine across their fields. The combine picks up the wheat and separates the grain from the straw. Workers sometimes bale the straw to use it as bedding for cattle. The wheat kernels are loaded up on a truck and hauled to a grain elevator for storage.

There the grain is tested for quality. Higher quality wheat is made into flour and pasta, while low-grade grain is used for cattle feed. The better the quality, the higher the price farmers can get for their grain.

Service people make up 73 percent of the province's workforce. Some are doctors, teachers, or bankers. Others have jobs in tourism. Tourists hike through Prince Albert National Park and visit the historic sites that dot every corner of Saskatchewan. Service workers in resorts and in restaurants help these travelers enjoy their stay.

About 6 percent of the workers in Saskatchewan have jobs in manufacturing. Some of them work in food-processing plants, where they grind wheat into flour, make cooking oil from seed crops, and package meat and dairy products. Many factory workers in the province produce fertilizers or other chemicals used on farms. At Saskatchewan's mills, employees saw timber into building materials, poles, and fence posts.

Some researchers in Saskatchewan look for new and better ways of processing foods.

Loggers, who harvest trees for wood products, make up only a small part of the province's workforce. Most loggers cut down trees in forests north of Prince Albert. To make sure the forests survive, officials have passed laws placing limits on how many trees loggers can fell. These workers also plant new seedlings on cleared land. By managing the woods, forestry workers can ensure that enough trees will be left for future generations.

Northerners also must follow laws that have been passed to protect certain kinds of wildlife. Hunters, for example, can kill only a limited number of geese and ducks. Restrictions also have been placed on the amount of fishing and trapping done in the province.

Workers in the logging industry (top) ***use chain saws to cut down trees. Officials in the province*** (bottom) ***inspect the loggers' work.***

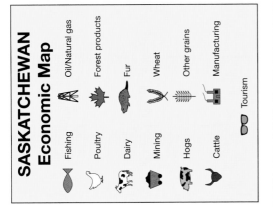

SASKATCHEWAN
Economic Map

Fishing		Oil/Natural gas	
Poultry		Forest products	
Dairy		Fur	
Mining		Wheat	
Hogs		Other grains	
Cattle		Manufacturing	
		Tourism	

The symbols on this map show where different economic activities take place in Saskatchewan. The map's legend in the box to the upper right explains what each symbol stands for.

49

About 2 percent of the province's workers have jobs in mining. But Saskatchewan has rich mineral resources and makes a lot of money from the industry. Miners dig up gold, silver, copper, uranium, and zinc in the northern areas of the province. Natural gas, coal, and oil are valuable resources, too. In Regina and Lloydminster, workers at special plants called upgraders process heavy oil into fuel.

Another important mineral is potash, a crumbly ore. Potash is valuable as a key ingredient in fertilizer. Saskatchewan's mines produce about 90 percent of Canada's potash. Experts in Saskatchewan believe that the province has enough potash to last thousands of years.

Saskatchewan's minerals can't be replaced after they are used up. To make sure that the province's mineral supplies last, mining companies are careful to collect minerals efficiently. The companies also are required to clean up areas that they have mined. By restoring the land and replanting grass and trees, these firms help preserve Saskatchewan's natural beauty.

Pumps pull oil from wells along the plains. Saskatchewan is Canada's second largest oil-producing province after Alberta.

Officials in the province are trying to increase manufacturing jobs (left) *so that Saskatchewan can rely less on farming* (below).

Saskatchewan's leaders hope that mining, logging, tourism, and manufacturing will play an even bigger role in the province's future. That way Saskatchewan's economy won't depend as heavily on farming. But the Wheat Province will remain famous for its endless prairies and rippling fields of golden grain.

Knee-deep in wildflowers, horses carry riders across the rolling hills of southwestern Saskatchewan.

More Than Farmers

When you think of Saskatchewan, you might imagine farmers and small towns. But the province also has big cities, a rugged northland, and a population made up of people from many different backgrounds.

Many of the province's one million people have British, German, or Ukrainian roots. Others have a Scandinavian, French, Polish, or Dutch heritage. People of Asian or African descent also call the province home. A large number of Indians and Métis have chosen to remain in Saskatchewan, close to their homelands.

Of all the people in Saskatchewan, Indians are the fastest-growing group. Many Aboriginals in the province share music, dance, food, and friendship at large gatherings called powwows.

Young people take a break at a powwow.

About half of the Aboriginals in Saskatchewan live on reserves, located mostly in rural areas around the province. Some of these families have farms or ranches. Other Indians live and work in cities and take classes at the Saskatchewan Indian Federated College in Regina.

English is Saskatchewan's official language, but some residents speak other languages, such as Ukrainian, German, French, and Cree. Some French-speakers in Saskatchewan live in Gravelbourg, a town located southwest of Regina. Many descendants of Ukrainian and German settlers make their homes in rural areas where their ancestors originally settled.

Most people in Saskatchewan live in the southern part of the province.

Cities in the region include Regina, North Battleford, Swift Current, Prince Albert, and Estevan. The largest city, Saskatoon, boasts the University of Saskatchewan, a school known for its research in agriculture and medicine. Moose Jaw, another southern city, is home to a Canadian armed forces base and a famous aerobatics team—the Snowbirds. The Snowbirds perform fancy dives as they fly their planes across Saskatchewan's skies.

Sitting on the banks of the South Saskatchewan River, Saskatoon is nicknamed the City of Bridges. Farther south, in the town of Moose Jaw, Snowbird planes (inset) *are ready for takeoff.*

Small farming communities dot Saskatchewan's Plains region. Many of these settlements have a grain elevator, a gas station, a school, and a few small stores. Residents often gather at a local arena to enjoy sporting events and community suppers, especially after harvest or during the winter.

Farm families drive to Saskatchewan's larger towns to shop, get medical care, or attend special events. A favorite outing is the Canadian Western Agribition, held each fall in Regina. This agricultural fair is a major livestock sale, where ranchers and farmers auction off cattle, hogs, and other animals. Tourists often watch this well-known event.

Whether they live in small towns or big cities, many people in Saskatchewan celebrate the province's mix of cultures.

At the popular Vesna Festival in Saskatoon, Ukrainian dancers wearing traditional dresses entertain crowds of people.

Folkfest in Saskatoon highlights ethnic foods and handmade crafts. Regina's Mosaic, a three-day celebration, showcases the music and dance of various cultures. At yearly festivals, Ukrainians perform the songs of their homelands, and Polish dancers wear fancy traditional costumes.

Ethnic groups in Saskatchewan also celebrate their traditions at home. Chinese residents, for example, honor the Chinese New Year in late January or in February. Ukrainians celebrate Christmas and Easter later than other Canadians do. Decorating fancy Easter eggs is a famous Ukrainian tradition—no two eggs look the same!

Aboriginal history is honored near Saskatoon at Wanuskewin Heritage Park, whose name comes from a Cree word that means "seeking peace of mind." At the park, visitors hike past old buffalo kill sites and examine ancient Indian artifacts.

The province has many artists with unique talents. Their artworks are displayed in galleries and museums or sold at local craft fairs. Actors and dancers in Saskatchewan perform at theaters throughout the province, including Regina's Globe Theatre. Music lovers flock to Big Valley Jamboree in Craven, where international country-music stars entertain each year.

An Indian artist shows a group how to make a dream catcher—an artwork designed to ward off bad dreams.

In Saskatchewan, people young and old enjoy snowshoeing (above) **and canoeing** (facing page).

Residents of Saskatchewan explore the great outdoors at the province's many parks. Favorite activities include camping, fishing, and nature watching as well as cross-country skiing and snowmobiling during colder months. People in Saskatchewan also love to golf—and why not, since the province has more golf courses per person than anywhere else in North America!

Many residents enjoy curling, a game in which players slide a stone across the ice to reach a target. Students in elementary schools even take curling lessons. Saskatchewan's hockey fans follow the fortunes of Western Hockey League teams in several towns. And football lovers cheer for the Saskatchewan Roughriders, of the Canadian Football League.

Compared to most other Canadian provinces, Saskatchewan has a small population and few large cities. But the province boasts many big achievements. Throughout its history, Saskatchewan's hardworking and skilled people have strived to farm the land well and to prosper. Saskatchewan was built, as its motto states, from many peoples' strength.

Famous Saskatchewanians

1 **Archibald Belaney** (1888–1938) is better known as Grey Owl. At age 17, he moved from England to northern Canada, where he convinced people across the nation that he was part Indian—probably because of his early fascination with Aboriginal peoples. Grey Owl wrote many popular books about land conservation and became a park ranger at Prince Albert National Park in Saskatchewan.

Max Braithwaite (1911–1995) was a humor writer from Nokomis, Saskatchewan. His most famous book, *Why Shoot the Teacher?*, describes his experience teaching during the Depression and was made into an award-winning movie.

3 **Maria Campbell** (born 1940) is a playwright and author from Batoche, Saskatchewan. Her best-selling autobiography, *Halfbreed*, describes growing up as a Métis during the 1950s. In the 1970s, the book sparked a new interest in Métis and Indian cultures.

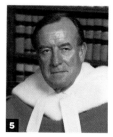

4 **Ethel Catherwood** (1909–1987) was an athlete who grew up in Saskatoon. Nicknamed the Saskatoon Lily, Catherwood won the gold medal in the women's running high jump competition during the 1928 Olympics.

5 **Brian Dickson** (born 1916), from Yorkton, Saskatchewan, was a lawyer before becoming Chief Justice of the Supreme Court of Canada in 1984. Dickson played an important role in interpreting the Canadian Charter of Rights and Freedoms through his court decisions and judgments.

6 **John G. Diefenbaker** (1895–1979), Canada's 13th prime minister from 1957 to 1963, moved to Saskatoon at a young age. He attended the University of Saskatchewan before becoming a well-known lawyer and politician in the province. A popular leader, Diefenbaker helped launch the Canadian Bill of Rights, which recognizes Canadian peoples' rights to liberty and personal security.

7 **Gabriel Dumont** (1837–1906) was born in a Métis settlement in the Red River area of Saskatchewan. A hunter and soldier, he led the Métis during the North-West Rebellion of 1885. He later escaped to the United States and joined Buffalo Bill's Wild West Show as a target shooter.

■ **Joseph Fafard** (born 1942) is famous for his ceramic, plaster, and bronze sculptures of people and animals. His work *The Pasture,* of seven bronze cows, stands outside the IBM Tower in downtown Toronto, Ontario. Fafard was born in Sainte-Marthe-Rocanville, Saskatchewan.

9 **Sylvia Fedoruk** (born 1927) from Canora, Saskatchewan, is a nuclear physicist. A pioneer in radiation therapy, she helped patients at the Saskatoon Cancer Clinic. In 1988 she became the first woman in the province to hold the position of lieutenant-governor.

10 **Gordie Howe** (born 1928), a record-holding hockey player, has won many awards, including the Art Ross Trophy and the Hart Trophy. A National Hockey League all-star 21 times, this outstanding athlete played for the Detroit Red Wings and the Hartford Whalers. Born in Floral, Saskatchewan, Howe retired from the professional sport at age 52.

■ **Frances Hyland** (born 1927) is an international actress from Shaunavon, Saskatchewan, who was trained in London, England. She has performed on Broadway, for television and movies, and in Shakespearean plays at the Stratford Festival in Ontario.

61

12 Colin James (born 1964) was introduced to folk and blues music at a young age in his hometown of Regina. In the 1980s, this award-winning blues singer and guitarist released his first album, and he has continued recording.

13 Art Linkletter (born 1912) was adopted in Moose Jaw, Saskatchewan, and moved to the United States with his new parents. During World War II, Linkletter was a well-known radio personality and found continued success writing and producing radio shows. He later penned many humor books, including *Kids Say the Darndest Things*.

14 Rueben Mayes (born 1963), from North Battleford, Saskatchewan, was a star running back for the New Orleans Saints football team. Voted Rookie of the Year in 1986, he went on to play briefly with the Seattle Seahawks and has since announced his retirement from the sport.

15 Violet McNaughton (1879–1968) was born in England and moved to Saskatchewan, where she became involved in women's rights issues. In 1915 she formed the Saskatchewan Equal Franchise League, which helped women in the province gain the right to vote. McNaughton continued working for women's causes as a national feminist leader.

16 Ken Mitchell (born 1940), a teacher from Moose Jaw, Saskatchewan, has written plays, novels, and short stories—many of which explore the people of the prairies. His interest in examining prairie life led him to edit a collection called *Horizon: Writings of the Canadian Prairie*.

17 W. O. Mitchell (born 1914) is a writer from Weyburn, Saskatchewan. His classic 1947 novel, *Who Has Seen the Wind,* portrays life on the windy prairie. Mitchell's radio plays about the eccentric members of an imaginary small town in the province were popular during the 1950s and later led to a television program.

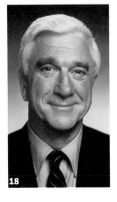

18 **Leslie Nielsen** (born 1926) is from Regina and now lives in California, where he is a famous comic actor. Nielsen has appeared in many television shows and movie comedies, including the film *The Naked Gun* and its sequels, in which he portrays a bumbling police detective.

19 **Ernie Richardson** (born 1931) from Stoughton, Saskatchewan, is a curling champion and has written many books about the sport. During the 1950s and 1960s, Richardson led the famous Richardson Rink—four-time winners of the international Scotch Cup—to many victories.

20 **Buffy Sainte-Marie** (born 1941), a folk singer, was born on the Piapot Reserve in Saskatchewan. She grew up in the United States, where she joined New York's folk-music scene and eventually gained world fame. She is well-known for her war protest song "The Universal Soldier" and for her support of Indian issues.

21 **Allen Sapp** (born 1929), considered one of Canada's leading painters, is famous for his oil paintings that show the daily life of the Plains Cree during the 1930s and 1940s. Born on the Red Pheasant Reserve, he later moved to North Battleford, Saskatchewan, where he pursued his career as a professional artist.

22 **Jeanne-Mathilde Sauvé** (born 1922) worked as a journalist in television and radio, with a focus on women's issues, before turning to politics. Born in Prud'homme, Saskatchewan, Sauvé was elected as Speaker of the House of Commons in 1980. Four years later, she was appointed Governor General of Canada.

63

Fast Facts

Provincial Symbols

Motto: *Multis E Gentibus Vires*
(From many peoples' strength)
Nicknames: Canada's Breadbasket, Wheat Province
Flower: western red lily (also known as prairie lily)
Tree: white birch
Bird: sharp-tailed grouse
Tartan: gold for prairie wheat, brown for summer fallow, green for the forests, red for the western red lily, yellow for rapeseed and sunflowers, white for snow, and black for oil, coal, and mineral wealth

Provincial Highlights

Landmarks: Fort Walsh in the Cypress Hills, Moose Jaw Wild Animal Park, Royal Canadian Mounted Police Training Center in Regina, the Great Sand Hills and the Big Muddy Badlands in southern Saskatchewan, Wanuskewin Heritage Park near Saskatoon

Annual events: International Kite Festival in Regina (June), Frontier Days Regional Fair and Rodeo in Swift Current (June–July), Big Valley Jamboree in Craven (July), Buffalo Days in Regina (Aug.), Western Canada Amateur Old Tyme Fiddling Championships in Swift Current (Sep.), Champion Dog Derby in Prince Albert (Feb.), Canadian Western Agribition (Nov.–Dec.)

Professional sports team: Saskatchewan Roughriders (football)

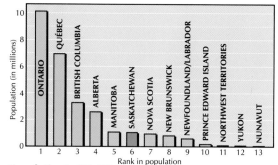

Population*: 989,000
Rank in population, nationwide: 6th
Population distribution: 63 percent urban; 37 percent rural
Population density: 4.5 people per sq mi (1.7 per sq km)
Capital: Regina (179,178)
Major cities (and populations*): Saskatoon (188,840), Prince Albert (34,181), Moose Jaw (34,130), Yorkton (15,315), Swift Current (14,815), Estevan (10,240)
Major ethnic groups*: multiple backgrounds, 51 percent; British, 17 percent; German, 12 percent; Aboriginals, 7 percent; Ukrainian, 6 percent; French, 3 percent; Scandinavian, 2 percent; Dutch and Polish, 1 percent each

*1991 census

Endangered Species

Birds: anatum peregrine falcon, mountain plover, piping plover, sage thrasher
Plants: slender mouse-ear cress

Geographic Highlights

Area (land/water): 251,865 sq mi (652,330 sq km)
Rank in area, nationwide: 7th
Highest point: Cypress Hills (4,816 ft/1,468 m)
Major rivers: North and South Saskatchewan, Clearwater, Churchill, Qu'Appelle
Major lakes: Athabasca, Reindeer, Wollaston, Cree, Lac la Ronge, Peter Pond, Doré

Economy
Percentage of Workers Per Job Sector:

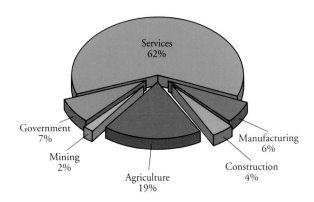

Services 62%

Government 7%

Mining 2%

Agriculture 19%

Construction 4%

Manufacturing 6%

Natural resources: fertile soils, uranium, copper, gold, silver, zinc, potash, oil, coal, sodium sulfate, salt, natural gas
Agricultural products: wheat, beef and dairy cattle, hogs, barley, canola, flaxseed, hay, mustard seed
Manufactured goods: food and beverage products, meat products, printed materials, chemicals, cement products, electrical equipment, machinery

Energy
Electric power: coal (75 percent), hydroelectric (20 percent), natural gas (5 percent)

65

10,000 B.C. Early peoples hunt in what is now Saskatchewan

1691 Henry Kelsey meets with Plains Indians

1821 Hudson's Bay Company expands

1754 Anthony Henday visits plains

1730s French build trading posts along Saskatchewan River

A.D. 800 Indian nations inhabit region

1774 Cumberland House is built

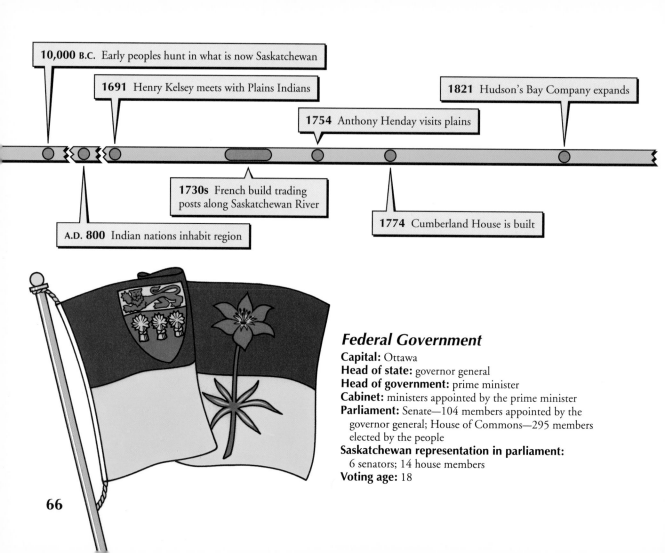

Federal Government

Capital: Ottawa
Head of state: governor general
Head of government: prime minister
Cabinet: ministers appointed by the prime minister
Parliament: Senate—104 members appointed by the governor general; House of Commons—295 members elected by the people
Saskatchewan representation in parliament: 6 senators; 14 house members
Voting age: 18

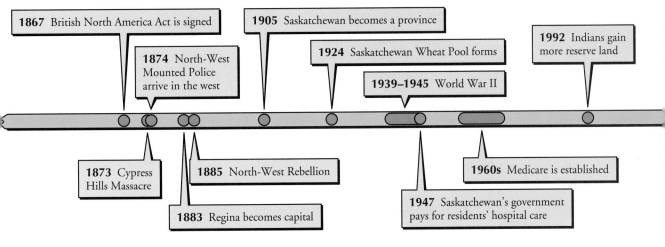

1867 British North America Act is signed

1874 North-West Mounted Police arrive in the west

1905 Saskatchewan becomes a province

1924 Saskatchewan Wheat Pool forms

1992 Indians gain more reserve land

1939–1945 World War II

1873 Cypress Hills Massacre

1885 North-West Rebellion

1960s Medicare is established

1883 Regina becomes capital

1947 Saskatchewan's government pays for residents' hospital care

Provincial Government

Capital: Regina
Head of state: lieutenant-governor
Head of government: premier
Cabinet: ministers appointed by the premier
Legislative Assembly: 64 members elected to terms that can last up to five years
Voting age: 18
Major political parties: Liberal, New Democratic, Progressive Conservative

Government Services

To help pay the people who work for Saskatchewan's government, people from Saskatchewan pay taxes on money they earn and on many of the items they buy. The services run by the provincial government help assure Saskatchewanians of a high quality of life. Government funds pay for medical care, for education, for road building and repairs, and for other facilities such as libraries and parks. In addition, the government has funds to help people who are disabled, elderly, or poor.

Glossary

drought   A long period of extreme dryness due to lack of rain or snow.

glacier   A large body of ice and snow that moves slowly over land.

hydropower   The electricity produced by using the force of flowing water. Also called hydroelectric power.

immigrant   A person who moves into a foreign country and settles there.

insecticide   A substance that kills insects.

pothole   A small depression in the land. After a rainstorm or when nearby snow melts, potholes fill up with water. In periods of hot and dry weather, the potholes often dry up.

prairie   A large area of level or gently rolling grassy land with few trees.

precipitation   Rain, snow, and other forms of moisture that fall to earth.

reserve   Public land set aside by the government to be used by Indians.

sanctuary   A place where hunting of wildlife is prohibited.

treaty   An agreement between two or more groups, usually having to do with peace or trade.

An artist in Saskatchewan proudly displays her work.

Pronunciation Guide

Aboriginal (a-buh-RIHJ-nuhl)

Assiniboine (uh-SIHN-uh-boyn)

Athabasca (ath-uh-BAS-kuh)

Chipewyan (chip-uh-WY-uhn)

La Vérendrye, Louis-Joseph Gaultier de (lah vay-rah^n-DREE, loo-EE joh-SEHF goh-tee-AY duh)

Métis (may-TEE)

Regina (rih-JY-nuh)

Riel, Louis (ry-EHL, loo-EE)

Saskatchewan (suh-SKATCH-uh-wawn)

Wanuskewin (wah-nuhs-KAY-wihn)

Index

Saskatchewan Roughriders

About the Author

Gillian Richardson has been a teacher-librarian in Canadian elementary schools since 1972. A writer of children's books and articles for juvenile magazines, Richardson is a member of the Saskatchewan Writer's Guild and the Canadian Society of Children's Authors, Illustrators, and Performers. She and her husband live in Regina.

Acknowledgments

Laura Westlund, pp. 1, 3, 66–67; Karpan Photo, pp. 2, 7, 8–9, 14, 15, 16, 17 (both), 18, 19, 21 (both), 23 (bottom), 29, 42, 44, 45, 46, 47, 52, 53, 55 (large), 56, 59; Terry Boles, pp. 6, 12, 49, 65 (bottom left); David Dvorak, Jr., pp. 10, 11, 28; Mapping Specialists Limited, pp. 12, 13, 49; Gerry Lemmo, p. 23 (top); Confederation Life Gallery of Canadian History, pp. 24, 34–35; Hudson's Bay Company Archives, Provincial Archives of Manitoba, p. 25; James Ford Bell Library, University of Minnesota, p. 26; Saskatchewan Archives Board, pp. 27 (R–B 1563), 32 (R–A492–2), 34 (R–A2294), 37 (R–B215–5), 38 (R–B171–1), 39 (R–B9523), 40 (R–A7923), 61 (top left/R–B4008), 62 (bottom left/R–B5366–10), 63 (top right/59–952–01, bottom left/R–A27127); Glenbow Archives, Calgary, Alberta, pp. 30 (550–18), 61 (top right/NA–1063–1), 62 (middle left/NA–280–6); National Archives of Canada, pp. 33 (PA138573), 35 (PA28853); Industry, Science, and Technology Canada Photo, pp. 41, 43, 51 (top), 58, 69; Government of Saskatchewan, Photographic Services Agency, pp. 48 (both), 50, 61 (bottom right); Saskatchewan Agriculture & Food, p. 51 (bottom); Jerry Hennen, p. 55 (inset); *Saskatoon Star-Phoenix,* p. 57; Archives of Ontario, p. 60 (top left/AO 2828); Greg Young-ing, p. 60 (middle left); Brian Dickson's Office, p. 60 (middle right); Canada's Sports Hall of Fame, p. 60 (bottom); *Brantford Expositor,* p. 61 (bottom left); James O'Mara, p. 62 (top left); SportsChrome East/West, Jeff Carlick, p. 62 (middle right); StarPhoenix Photo, p. 62 (bottom left); Hollywood Book & Poster, pp. 62 (top right), 63 (top left); EMI Music Canada, p. 63 (middle); Sgt. Bertrand Thibeault, Rideau Hall, p. 63 (bottom right); Royal Studios/Saskatchewan Roughriders, p. 72.